DAYS FROM MY WALK
A COLLECTION OF POETRY

BY
SHARYN HILLS

A Sunset Pointe Press Book

Publishing History
August, 2018 Trade Paperback

Published by Sunset Pointe Press
Atlanta, GA

All Rights Reserved
Copyright © 2015 by Sharyn Hills

Author Photo, Stacey S. Hamilton
for Stace.H. Photography

Original Cover Artwork:
Sharyn Hills

Senior Editor, Katherine Thornton for Sunset Pointe Press

Library of Congress Card Catalogue Number on File

ISBN 978-0-9838208-6-4

Printed in the United States of America

DAYS FROM MY WALK
A COLLECTION OF POETRY

BY
SHARYN HILLS

Atlanta, GA

DEDICATION

This book is dedicated to Those GOD has placed in my life, and to them that came with Them. For without you ALL, I would not believe as I do.

Table of Contents

9 - I See
10 - Talkin' to God
11 - Untitled 1
12 - Untitled 2
13 - Chosen
14 - Circumstances
15 - I Worry Not
16 - A Testament of Faith
17 - To My Sister
18 - A Conversation With God
22 - The Abundance of God's Grace
23 - Untitled 3
24 - Untitled 4
25 - The Ultimate Price
26 - Habbakkuk 2:14
27 - *September 14, 2006*
28 - Untitled 5
29 - Untitled 6
30 - *September 15, 2006*
31 - Who Be You?
32 - I'm Supposed to Be Here
33 - Victory
34 - Hearken
35 - It's My Season
36 - The Trial of Faith
37 - Complacency
38 - The Firsts
39 - To My Dear Mother
40 - This Is My Faith
43 - A Measure of Faith
44 - The First Silence
45 - Untitlted 6
46 - Untitled 7
47 - The Right Path
48 - In God We (Should) Trust
49 - IT

50 - This Week and Next
51 - The Practicality of Faith
52 - The Wet Devil's Reply
53 - Revived!
54 - How I Believe
56 - At Beautiful
57 - That Which I Seek
58 - I AM Her
59 - YOUR Messengers
60 - *June 23, 2007*
61 - The Reason for the Season
63 - Pacts With God
64 - Jesus Said - (Complacency Part II)
65 - Unlawful - ?
66 - IT Too
67 - Untitled 8
68 - Useful Idiots
69 - Our Shoes
70 - Jesus Had to Pray
73 - The Battlefield
74 - Under the Lily Whites
75 - Anyoneofus - Prodigal Children
76 - In Beginnings
79 - And I Know I Know
82 - An Agape Type of Thing
83 - Duality - More Than ONE - Equal to Two
85 - HOPE Laid Up
87 - NOW
89 - Measured Distance
91 - *November 17. 2010*
93 - Complete Faith

I See
June 30, 2006

I've always known I could see in others
What others couldn't or didn't themselves see
Good and/or bad, I let my gift be
Hidden for so long, but now I see the real me
I praise GOD because I see
It wasn't him but HE

HE sent love to set us free – I see
Stronger our lone selves are we
To get to where we ought to be
Both with HIM our separate ways

I see also GOD's love never fades.

Talkin' to GOD
July 31, 2006

I've been talkin' to GOD, but for only a few days
Never forgettin' to give HIM praise, for being HE
As well as for what HE's given me

I – one lost for so long – within and by myself – lone
Sometimes I've felt I'm too far gone
For HIM to claim me as one of HIS own
Those feelings they twist me up inside
For while I sought HIS word – I've tried to hide
Not from HIM, my faith nor my devotion,
Just a race in which I've no trust in.

So I've been talkin' to GOD, but for only a few days
Never forgettin' to give HIM praise, for being HE
As well as for all HE's done for me –
Protection from myself and the race,
And the wisdom to know it's time to show my faith.

Untitled 1
August 12, 2006

Those sins of the past that's where they stay
Once you accept Christ and walk in His way
First a hunger, you just can't feed
So go to church and the bible a must read
Sooner or later the doubt will creep in
A product of desire and/or non-faith of family or friend
Just call on the Lord and He'll bring peace within
And say to the devil – "Get thee behind me Satan"   Matt 4:10
And as you feel your doubt slip away
Wave to GOD and by all means pray
Thank GOD, and ask for strength of faith and conviction
'Cause once in GOD's will, Satan makes you a mission.

Untitled 2
August 12, 2006

A call to all saints, that's what I read
When I open the bible to nourish the seed
The seed of GOD's Spirit which brings about faith
Faith in GOD and in you too
To get done those things HE wills you to do
Unsure of your gifts, by all means self assess
And look to GOD to bring forth your best
It's hard sometimes as all saints know
But ask for direction and HE'll tell you how to go

Chosen
August 20, 2006

For a long time it used to be
I didn't know who I be
Confused by so called friends and family
Of which now I never and hardly see
Unsure of myself and the blood in my veins
My spirit collapsed under the strain
I turned from GOD and took root in myself
And lived my life in somewhat stealth
Never letting anyone get to know the real me
I wore the masks people wanted to see
By myself it was unknown – that I was never left alone
For GOD still saw me as one of HIS own
By way of HIS mercy and I praise HIM for that
'Cause after 30 plus years it's me coming back
Now I know just who I be
I'm a chosen one of HE
For as this poem is just a part of me
I praise GOD for the rest shall see
The will of GOD has rescued me.

Circumstances
August 23, 2006

Made unhappy by circumstance
Not of GOD but of what HE's created
Mankind in the likeness of HIM
Not knowing without HIM I can't win
I turned not to GOD but within

Look at me now in poorness and unhealth
Ashamed of me and my mental health
What I fear besides HIM –
Is I'm too late and my mental state
Depressed to the point I wish I were dead
Never wondering why I've kept my head
I'm tired now and want not to go on
And hope when HE takes me it's by quiet storm

Needing so much and wanting so little
I don't seem to locate the middle
For every time I take one forward
Circumstance makes it out as froward
But I'm of GOD's will now or at least try to be
Praying in Christ's name and unwanting of fame
Praying me and all mankind be free
To experience the fullness of the love of HE.

I Worry Not
August 24, 2006

I worry not what tomorrow will bring
For I know the Lord GOD sees all things
As for my past I know HE was there
Making sure I got my proportionate share
Never did I thank HIM or praise HIS name
No doubt the reason for my current shame
So take from someone it took to long to learn
It's of GOD's will you should be concerned.

Still I worry not what tomorrow will bring
For I know the Lord GOD sees all things
As for my present – I know HE's here
For it's by HIS grace I put this down
Able to express the freedom I've found
Trusting in HIM with all my heart .
And the wisdom to know from me HE won't part.

A Testament of Faith
August 24, 2006

Steadfast and no longer lost
I'm more than willing to pay HIS cost
To get to GOD and within HIS will
I forgave all evil which pinned me in
Confessed the Lord Christ as well as my sins
And believe now with all my heart and might
That GOD will and sees fit to spare my life
For as I stand in the midst of my correction
I can't fathom a change in my direction
For I am in a race that I shall win
'Cause within me GOD's Spirit won't give in
Meekened I get on my knees
And pray that in me HE may be pleased
For as the pace quickens I keep up
Pride and selfishness I've given up
I give as and what I can and offer myself
For besides me I have nothing else
Humbled now but not despaired
I wait for GOD to answer my prayers.

To My Sister
August 24, 2006

To my sister
Who's not yet aware
Some poetry I now must share
Bestowed unto me from above
A gift of GOD's unfailing love
My fledgling testament of my faith
As well as confirmation as we wait
While GOD unfurls HIS plans for me
I shall stay on bended knee

    ***

To my loving sister who shares my concern
I pray you not worry for I've truly learned
GOD is with me and from HIM I'll not turn
    For as I stand in the midst of my correction
    I can't fathom a change in my direction
    As I am in a race that I shall win
    Because within me GOD's Spirit won't give in
So worry not that I may be lost
For I assure you that I've picked up my cross

While circumstance sometimes chokes my air
I turn to GOD, the bible and say my prayers
And when I'm done – I have peace within
So worry not what tomorrow will bring
For I know GOD sees and hears everything

Just a couple things before I sign this off
I'm sure in you GOD must really be pleased
And I never forget to mention you when I'm on my knees.

A Conversation With GOD
August 27, 2006

My measure of faith
It was for me a perplexing thing
I pray GOD prove me as I put this down
The measure in which I do abound
For HE knows my heart and guides my pen
As it's just one of the ways
I may communicate with HIM…

I first gave each the same measure
It is the ways of man that diminish the treasure
For there was a moment in your life you did shine
As MY Spirit in you told you "the world is MINE"…

No one in this life had to tell me it ain't easy
Nor did anyone tell me they'd do me sleazy
I found these things early and on my own
And by the age of nine I felt completely alone
At the time the Ten Commandments were barely known
Then "GOD don't like ugly" was driven home
With the "sins of my fathers were my own"
The world did cover GOD's seed sown

They preached to you that you are sin
Not knowing you are already privy to the evils of men
MY milk not enough to feed the spirit within
MY shine in you did grow dim…

Acceptance of all the blame
Of the sins committed against and in my name
Gave birth to an inward shame
Remembrance of all innocence lost
Gave way to a self destructive course

Yea, MY light in you was only a glimmer
But and because – hope did simmer
The wisdom of ME in you was sown
And throughout the years it had grown
Even as you tried to hide from the world
You sought ME and didn't know
For the abundance of love that I have given you
You demonstrated to some you barely knew
Another blessing unto you…

Deep inside I knew I was not like them
I only longed for a good friend
Someone I could completely trust in
But my mouth was sewn shut in and by the world
And whispers of all who thought me they knew
And out of that a new self awareness grew
Along with my motto – "I'll do me, you do you."

Yea, you were in a season, but hearkened not to ME
Had you been diligent in seeking ME
You would now know what your true blessings be

The recesses of my heart and mind I searched
To find what drives me on this earth
It's not anything I can put my hands on
As I care not what others have, think or say
Discontented I kept my way

Your way wrong!
You attempt to destroy MY temple
Thou art corrupt by the wayside of your own kind
Yea, your mind attempts to corrupt the goodness of your own heart
There in you must be a new start;
Behold, to you that which you seek…

Emotionally corrupt – I care not for any
Unless they somehow entertain me
The internet; a new device

And on it I can be cold as ice
No change in me, until that day
That dude Gokon came my way

This one, but not yet!
There are things you need to remember and forget
You know all vengeance is MINE own rite
But you yourself must forgive
This one, but not yet, that you may live…

And then
I hear it – "This one, but not yet!"
It swallows me whole
I can't explain it, but it takes control
He's only 18, what is it, I can't see?
I can't let it go, as the vibe's a part of me.

For four years "This one, but not yet!"
Take from it and turn it in
See those things that pin you in
And unseal your heart,
And from it a brand new start.

It's not what you both may think
But both are the key, by which your spirits shall be set free
Take what you need, both are willing
Give back as you have to give, and both shall live
Remain true to what you have found in MY good Spirit
And before it's over, you both shall hear it…

Nine months since our last chat
It's February 2006
And a kink in the vibe must be fixed
A 'hey hun, where you been?'
Along with a cry of lets talk again
A simple email nothing more
And it was GOD who opened doors

It is because of the goodness in your heart
You did from you path depart
Remove yourself from the other and be blessed
As the fruit of your spirit be MY words
Write them down and we both be heard.

The Abundance of GOD's Grace
August 28, 2006
Psalm 36:5-7

HIS mercy as vast as the heavens
HIS faithfulness the same
HIS righteousness solid as a mountain range
HE looks after the righteous and the wicked too
For as promised to Noah, that be true   Gen 9:11, 12
How excellent is the love of GOD?
This is how I see…

Unto us are gifts from above
Given to us as an expression of GOD's unfailing love
A love as pure and as vast as arctic ice
Bestowed upon us before we knew life
Those who seek HIM early, are truly blessed
But that doesn't mean latecomers less
HIS forgiveness more powerful than any of our sins
And within each one of us is a part of HIM

So as we the children of man put our trust in the LORD
We will abundantly reap our rewards
HIS judgments are a great deep, but that's as a whole
For as we're called before HIM, they're as deep as our souls.

Untitled 3
September 7, 2006

Even as life's issues should have me stressed
I know by GOD I'm truly blessed
Out of work and UI's run out
I'm blessed by GOD of this I've no doubt
Landlord's threatening my eviction
Yet and still I keep my faith and conviction
Ever close to my heart, because I know HIS love will never part

I look to GOD to ease my strife
And intercede on behalf of my life
I know HE hears me, for some have occurred
And as I pray, I search for the wisdom in HIS word
Enlightened and strengthened evermore by HIS touch
I really don't have to say to much
For GOD worked with me before I realized
Once aware I was re-baptized

Untitled 4
September 10, 2006

The happiest day is not of a time in my life
However, I acknowledged it
When I chose to follow Christ
As He is the way, the truth, and the life   John 14:6
I do as He would and end most of my strife

Jesus having been lifted up from this earth
Calls for us to experience a spirit of rebirth
By Him is the only way
A soul may survive on judgment day

His truth – I myself will attest –
There's only one GOD
And a life in HIS will, shall be blessed

Christ's life?
Well sometimes easier said than done
But repentance gives chance in chances
Not just one.

The Ultimate Prize
September 10, 2006

GOD spared Noah – Who was just?
And in doing so, HE spared us
Man created in the likeness of HIM
Inherently wicked and prone to sin
GOD's covenant unto man
Never again destroy all the land

HE later gave us HIS begotten Son
Now a choice to be made by everyone
Take Jesus Christ into your heart
Repent and with diligence do your part
Or lest you be wicked, and do as wicked does
For GOD has already shown you love

HE rewards you in your worldly life
And may have helped you surpass some strife
But remember – HE knew us before we did
And from HIM secrets can't be hid
And when judgment day besets us all
The righteous be the only to hear HIS call

Unto them the ultimate prize
Because heaven's not built on any lies.

Habakkuk 2:1-4
September 14, 2006

The righteous live by their faith   Hab 2:4
To live is Christ, and to die is gain   Phil 1:21

Have you sought GOD's face yet
Or do you really think HE forgets?

Is your soul and faith in tact,
Or does your mouth and heart lie?

Are you about GOD's commands
Or have you mischievous hands?

Do you do as GOD wills you to
Or really give the devil his due?

Can you see what's coming
Or do you think righteousness a lie?

Are you prepared to go before HIM
Or really think HIS judgment will pass you by?

September 14, 2006

"That ye may be blameless and harmless, the sons of God without rebuke, in the midst of a crooked and perverse nation, among whom ye shine as lights in the world;"
Philippians 2:15

In the sea of righteousness some of us have momentary lapses
Just don't forget GOD gives chances in chances
In a straight between the two
Go to church and do as Paul instructed the Philippians to do
Stand fast and in one Spirit and in one mind
And look to the gospel and your faith you'll find
Don't just read 1:27 – Read the entire book
So that all your situations may take on a joyous look
As GOD never allows what will make us fail
It's our faith in HIM that will bring wind to our sails.

Untitled 5
September 14, 2006

GOD since the inception of our time
Has shown HIS mercy throughout the bloodlines
HE who sacrificed HIS own Son
To show us how with HIM we may be ONE
Deserves not only the utmost praise
But also us as worldly slaves

Transform your mind and be of Christ
And wait as GOD transforms your life
Think not you better than your sister or brother
For all GOD's gifts are different from one another
Given to us to strengthen the body of Christ
As HIS measure increases, HE lessens your strife
What better reasons to HIM your life
As living, breathing sacrifice.

Hindsight
September 15, 2006

We are taught that hindsight is a virtue, but one must first live to
learn that its virtuous nature can only be
seen through the eyes of GOD.

Apparently GOD has called me several times
I unfortunately was too deaf, dumb and blind
For as I check the wake of my life
GOD was there in all my strifes

In two instances I thought GOD was striking me
But now I see – it was really GOD rescuing me
During my marriage I lost children – three
Better to GOD is now how I see
For my ex was not an upright man
And would have stolen them to take to his native land

From that I wouldn't have recovered me
For it was hard enough losing them to HE
I thank GOD rescuing me
Because I know again, I'll see all three

September 15, 2006

"Be strong and of a good courage, fear not, nor be afraid of them: for the Lord thy God, he it is that doth go with thee; he will not fail thee, nor forsake thee."

Deuteronomy 31:6

GOD's unfailing love
The ultimate gift from above
Who but GOD would send his son
To satisfy the evil one

If GOD willing satisfaction to the devil
Why not to faith of any level
Put your trust in GOD, and be not slack
And GOD will forever have your back.

Who Be You?
September 19, 2006

Who be you who judges or measures my way
That you may point your finger and say "Nay!"
You who is among men, and is seen and heard
Should not dare utter a judgmental word
For you be guilty found, but not by me
As I leave all judgments up to HE.
HE be my GOD – Righteous and above all
And I answer only to HIM, each and every time HE calls

So worry not for my faith, but that of your own
Because of your judgment you'll have to atone
And not just for speaking out of the side of your mouth
But for the audacity of thinking you had HIS clout

You think you better, well then cast your lot
For I may prove all from HIM I've got
While not as well versed in verse yet
GOD's works in me, shall definitely get
Silence from anyone who tries to rule me out
For my GOD be the only GOD
And this I don't doubt!

I'm Supposed To Be Here
September 20, 2006

I know all to well GOD watches me from above
For it's by HIS mercy and grace I receive HIS love
If not for GOD, I know this be true
I'd be six feet farther away from HIM
And under you

With that stated, I must move on
Before HIS judgment of me be upon
For there are things I've yet to say and do
And I'll do them willingly because HE wants me to

HE drives me in such a way, that I can't call it
I'm just thanking GOD that HE's my PILOT
My feet firmly embedded in HIS rock
If I ever go public, I'll buy my own stock
For HE assures me I'm as solid as HIS rock.

Victory
September 30, 2006

We are blessings upon the earth
Gifts of GOD and of worth
Blessings to all of mankind
For on that day no saints left behind
As we are of GOD THE FATHER
We're called to HIM and want not to wander
Some hear HIM sooner and others later
It doesn't really matter, for we all find HIS favor
For the moment we hear our name be called
Victory is celebrated by HIS saints one and all

Hearken
September 30, 2006

GOD loves you – so hearken to HIS voice
When you first hear HIM call your name
And look within your heart of hearts
And see you feel the same

GOD loves you – and just for you HIS will
Yet it you don't realize
So look within to GOD again
And watch it materialize

For nothing is a mystery
But only GOD can plainly see
For you a season has come about
As the proof be the fruit of your tree
And the unfailing love of HE

So seek HIM not for miracles
For you are one in the same
Just hearken to HIS voice
Every time HE calls your name

It's My Season
October 2, 2006

As I have come into a season
GOD has given me but some of HIS reason
HIS seed in me, planted by my mother
I left it, and the world did cover

My weeping and mourning now all done
For GOD has blessed me with a Son
The stones I used to pen in my strifes
HE's cast away, that I begin a new life

No longer do I embrace the 'old man'
But that of GOD's unfailing hand
And what I've given – it shant be missed
For my soul of heaven, it did kiss

As GOD knew me long before I ever did
And all about me I sought to keep hid
HE knew long ago, I in the world lost my voice
This pen in hand, be HIS new voice of choice
Given to me as only HE could
I pray all that see it – see GOD is good!

I am alive again because of HE
And the will of GOD has set me free
HE owns me now, mind, body and soul
Now everyone witness a love out of control.

The Trial of Faith
October 6, 2006

The trial of faith being more precious than gold   1 Pet 1:7
In accordance to the abundance of mercy GOD showed
Having heard our names called before death we found
Partake of HIS mercy and in life abound

Things I don't and shall never know at all
GOD's thoughts on whom and when HE calls
For GOD has known each before our birth
Knew some may cope better in the strifes of the earth
And knew others may need early to prove their worth
Which line called early and which one later?
It matters not, for in faith there's no hater
For the devil as real as Christ is and was
GOD has already shown man HIS love

The trial of faith that's more precious than gold
Be not of the 'old man' but that we live to be old.

Complacency
October 24, 2006

"Man shall not live by bread alone" Matt 4:4
Do you even realize what that means?
It further proves that GOD already knew our dreams
What will be judged on besides the Ten? Ex 20:1-17
Just how far out we're willing to go on faith's limb
Complacency is not a GOD-ly trait
Recognize before your bough breaks
Learn from someone who didn't see
For many years, GOD's correction of me
I praise GOD – For HE heard the cries of my soul
And told me HIS love never grows old
HE picked me up, and put me back in the race
And in me HE's quickened the pace
I'm counting my blessings in life unto now
In awe in the mystery in GOD's how
As for the why – all saints know
It's GOD's will that the body of Christ grow
HIS forgiveness and will greater than those of our own
Take a look at yourself and see all the seeds sown
For our lives are based on what's unfurled
On GOD's purpose of you in this world
To embrace GOD is to embrace your self
In accordance to the treasures of HIS Spirit – HE dealt
Give thanks and praise for what HE proves to you in this life
And reap benefit of and treasure in everlasting life

The Firsts
October 25, 2006

There are things in this life I don't understand
All to do with the ways of man
It's because of our ways we can't understand
The wisdom of GOD and the hour at hand
The foolishness of GOD that I do see
Is the extent, which HE's been forced to go
To prove HIS love of you and me.

Fear of GOD is the beginning of knowledge   Prov 1:7
To really understand that we don't need a degree
We only need to put ourselves in the presence of HE
If ever I'm asked what it is I think I see
My response will most assuredly be
The Word is GOD – GOD is the Word
GOD is GOD and I know all have heard

For GOD having created both heaven and earth
And all that is between – seen and unseen
And gave the breath of life to every human being
That being initially always all good
Alive and full of HIS good Spirit
Even as we age, we all still hear it
For every time we do something good
Not considering ourselves
It is GOD who is really showing HIMSELF

And if GOD's work in and through you
Isn't enough to put fear in you
I can tell you what I truly see…

The first will and word of GOD
Was that HE – BE!

To My Dear Mother
October 28, 2006

I pray you understand
I didn't realize GOD's will of life
Was at the heart of every man
For I had no faith nor trust of my own
Even though in me that seed you sewn
Hence my decision to send you home

I sorely miss you my dear mother
That I can't and won't deny
I pray also you forgive me the thorn in your side
As there are things I should have said
Before your season did pass me by

I should have thanked you for all you showed me
But I was blinded and couldn't see
So instead I blamed you for what others did
Years had gone by before I knew
A decision you made and hid wasn't for you
But for me I found and don't doubt
I realized that when Duncan sought me out

Now for and because of you my dear mother
I truly understand the wisdom of 'my father's sins be mine own'
For in the world your mouth was as my own
As it once used to be
For alas it's GOD I finally see
And HE's forgiven the silence of me
The proof of that be in the fruit of my tree
And HIS forgiveness of you I also see

Know dear mother if I had known the power of prayer
Your soul then would not have disturbed the air.

This Is My Faith
October 2006 – December 2006

I have found as I have dwelt in GOD's word
The notion to each his own faith a bit absurd
I confess being new to a saving faith
But seed has been given that may be sown
So be it if my faith is my own

Would I be wrong if I believed
That GOD really wants to be seen
And not just by those with saving faith
But by all HE did create?

Save that thought for here is some seed
Stay if you care, and continue to read….

As believers we know all these be true
All men originate from the first two
GOD having created us, knew us before we did
And what's done in the dark in HIS light can't be hid
A righteous man has never been born
Save GOD's grace the virgin's son
Christ who is the way, the truth and the life
As we repent and are baptized, we learn to be as Christ

Which brings me to these questions that I may ask…

Did not Christ come to reconcile those who on Him believe?
Did not His arrival make repentance and baptism the order of the
    New Testament's day?
And whose sins besides ours did get nailed to the cross, so that all
    of mankind would not be lost?

Save those thoughts one and all, for there is more seed
Stay if you care, and continue to read…

As I read through Genesis this I did see
There's no repentance at the root or beyond in our family's tree
In fact the only things that I did see
Was burnt offerings and GOD's mercy
Now as these things are written they are true
And cannot be disputed by me nor you
All men are sinful and fall short of the glory of HIM
And for four generations our father's sins be our own
And by GOD's mercy, many have passed
Thus the addition of sin to sin also passed

Which brings me to these questions that I may ask…

Knowing people as we do, and that includes me and you
In the generations since Christ,
How many people would you dare to say
Repented the sins of their great-great-grandfather's day?
And who among us can say who was of faith during those days
Or even what their measure was?

Which brings me back to Christ's cause and the will of GOD…

If Jesus is the Son of GOD,
Why does He refer to Himself as the Son of man?
Was it not so that we may see
That after we embrace Him we are as He?

Save those thoughts one and all, for here is the rest of the seed
Stay if you care and continue to read…

Now I confess that I haven't read the entire book
And Revelation beyond Chapter 2 deserves a closer look
For as I finished that last verse
I was moved to Daniel Chapter 2 – not of course
Therefore proving to me
That I'm to move through the word as He directs me
So that I may take closer looks and see
The many glorious faces of He
And I may be wrong, but in Ruth I did see

The Son of man before Christ came to be
For a dead man has no inheritance on earth
And the house of David was of Obed's birth.

With all this said this too I see
There's no middle ground with HE
The price of sin on earth is death
And as wrath filled vengeance belongs solely to GOD
Our vengeance upon our fellow man is hard
Forgiveness and repentance of all sins
Of which we all are inherently born in

Which brings me to these two truths
GOD commands that we honor both mother and father
And also made us keepers of one another

Of myself this I tell you,
As a near kinsman my faith belongs to you too
For GOD did so love the world
That HE sent HIS begotten Son
To show us how with HIM to be ONE
Redemption for those before and at Christ's cross
So that all of mankind on that day would not be lost
And GOD does so love the world still
As HIS will for us is of days
To name, claim, and repent our inherited ways
Joint heirs with Christ in heaven, and the cross
So that our father's inheritance in heaven be not lost
For if our faith would be completely our own
Then on that day, no mercy shown.

A Measure of Faith
November 9, 2006

A measure of faith is what you can in your heart believe
And it's all the more reason why you yourself should read
The bible taken to heart is GOD, the Spirit and the Son
All neatly packaged into one

Just as fear of GOD is the initial seed   Prov 1:7
Knowing GOD don't like ugly is why I began to read
And we can't get to the FATHER except through the Son
Which is why the church was begun
As Jesus Christ is the power and wisdom of GOD
For those who don't hear this life is hard
Since GOD's not promised anyone tomorrow to date
Best you accept the truth now, as you can be too late   2 Pet 3:10

GOD's power and wisdom combined guarantees new life
It's our measure of faith which determines the outcome of strife
GOD's power a miraculous gift to mankind
It's our measure of faith that brings strength in our daily grind
GOD's wisdom a living example to all with a saving faith
Read, believe, and wait, while you diligently seek GOD's face

My measure of faith is not mine own
Acceptance of and belief in Christ makes sure things shown
I praise GOD, as I repent and rebuke Satan in Christ's name
Surely in my life we both shall reign
For who is Christ but the King of kings
And together with Him I can do all things
And surely that means even one of those kings.

The First Silence
November 16, 2006

From the beginning, what I may see
The original sin could possibly be
The purposeful silence of the first Spiritual Truth
Buried deep within our family tree's roots

For it was that first silence
Which snowballed and gave cause to our ways
As evil matures in the mind where Satan still plays
For surely all men are holders of the divine truths
As we are all from the beginning of GOD's inspiration
It's the silence of many truths, which divided first HIS
Then many of our nations

And that first silence remains even unto this day
As our world leaders think it's better their way
That man should be so increasingly bold
Is a concept of man that never grows old

What is the first silence that I see
It's the truth that we could never be
Neither by one nor collectively
All GOD has proven HIMSELF to be.

Untitled 6
November 18, 2006

A believer in GOD's signs
That's who I be
And the end is near is what I see

As I was communing with GOD
And meditating on HIS word
It was the doorbell that I heard
And who should at my door be
But a Jehovah's Witness to share with me
"The End of False Religion is Near!'

That which I didn't share –
That concept was already under my hair

For what I know as GOD's words have shown me
There is no religion except it be by faith in HE
For all religious sects one thing is true
Your measure of faith doesn't belong to you
So you may listen to the preachers
The teachers, or whomever you see on TV
But I know what that truth of GOD be…

If you don't look for GOD yourself
HIS face to you will be forever in stealth.

Untitled 7
December 15, 2006

I live in a love of and not my own
One love that moved me from my comfort zone
It's lifted me unto heights I've never known
As well as given me a strength I can freely call on
HIS word of love draws me closer to HIM
It loosed my pen and freed my heart
And in life has given me a new start
I need only ask and I shall receive
HE loves me so much I get all I need
I worry no more, as I have found
The love of GOD cannot be bound

For as I've come full circle in life
Born again I fear no strife
As all my worry of what's not passed
Has now been up to GOD cast
And as HE shows me many a face
I'm ever more diligent in seeking HIS grace
Finding HIS truths and turning them on me
Shows me how HE meant us to be
Without Jesus we are all but pale
As Jesus is the Adam that didn't fail

The Right Path
December 23, 2006

Jealousy as you know – it is a sin
Thus beckons and welcomes Satan within
What for you care what the wicked has
You're blessed of GOD, and on HIS right path
A path unyielding and straight in the heart
And brings about new meaning to each day you start
For GOD didn't promise the world
HE just made it grow
And GOD didn't promise man
HE just out of the earth, formed him so
The goodness of GOD to man the seed
Enabled man to breathe and breed
Dominion over the earth met all man's needs
Of the flesh of Adam came Eve and greed
You're not satisfied with what you have
Best you look to your feet to ensure your path.

In GOD We (Should) Trust
December 26, 2006

In is HIM – HIM is GOD
In the beginning – GOD the beginning
See HE was before
Heavens and then the earth still void
By HIM and for HIM all things created
HIS order established!

GOD is GOD the FATHER
To all things given life
Out of nothing, HIS inspiration even prior to HIS light
Which transcends the heavens and the earth,
Our days and our nights
All the creatures of the seas, and earth
And last, but not least – Us of the dust

We, blessed by GOD since the beginning of our time
To us dominion and all seed
For without the breath of life from HE
Images in the mud is all we'd be
His love and will of days enough reason to praise
But both are excused as HIS order is reversed
With man putting himself first

Trust GOD first in all you do
For that is the order of HIS will
As HE was before all we've ever known
And HE will be even when all we've known is gone.

IT
2007

"And lest I should be exalted above measure through the abundance of the revelations, there was given to me a thorn in the flesh, the messenger of Satan to buffet me, lest I should be exalted above measure. For this thing I besought the Lord thrice, that IT might depart from me. And he said unto me, My grace is sufficient for thee: for my strength is made perfect in weakness. Most gladly therefore will I rather glory in my infirmities, that the power of Christ may rest upon me."

II Corinthians 12:7-9

IT is a physical anomaly
IT is an emotional catastrophe
IT is the unyielding flesh
By which the world and faith do mesh

IT is accusations by others
IT is things we can't or don't move from
Thus IT makes you wonder 'How come…?'

IT is our beliefs on who's right and/or wrong
IT is those beliefs that make us all wrong
IT is what we can't, don't, and won't see
On how others perceive us to be

Thus IT will cause us to harden our hearts
And can from saving faith to depart
IT has a sole purpose, we all must understand
IT is so we don't lose sight of GOD's unfailing hand.

This Week & Next
February 18, 2007

Don't give to the enemy all things or any
The blessings of GOD and there are plenty
As I have this week threatened to do
Only to realize I have more growth to put my mind to

My patience worn thin by a man's god on earth
And me with no time to show my GOD my worth
Hungry for my daily bread
My spirit's yearning to be fed
It's by the old man this week, I've been led
A mournful body and spirit each night I put to bed

Conversations with knowing and unknowing sisters and brothers
It was the wisdom of GOD I sought from others
And blessed with still the ability to help some others

It's the week's end and I'm finally able to pen
All the frustration I've held within
I pray in my Brother Jesus Christ's name
I remember next week from whence I came.

The Practicality of Faith
March 18, 2007

The power of prayer as witnessed by me
Is the power of GOD in all who see
The forgiveness, longsuffering, and reconciliation of HE

I practice it in Jesus' name
For therein is my hope to see
The all powerful, knowing, and glorious face of HE
In heaven, where we all hope to stay
On the coming of the Judgment Day

Which faith is right, which faith is wrong?
All are right and all are wrong!
As revelations make it clear to me
There's not one – and none are problem free

Practical application of the word
Self reflection is the word
For if I can't see me as GOD does see
At HIS throne I'll never be
With Jesus to the left of me.

The Wet Devil's Reply
May 3, 2007

You ever notice, when you step outside of your box
The people around you will start to talk
Some not knowing what they speak
'Cause hear it from you, they didn't seek
Try to explain it, but don't waste to much time
For a fool can't understand – GOD's Spirit is mine.

So I'll be that wet devil you see me to be,
But that's only as long as your judgment's upon me
For I know all that GOD promises me
And I intend to attain it you'll eventually see.

Revived!
May 8, 2007

I went to revival last night
And while there Satan put up a good fight
Stirring up old memories of 'dis' and 'non' association
So I only watched as my brother's and sister's made preparation
And just the day before I had wrote a line on GOD being amongst every nation

I didn't realize the 'old man' had come
Sitting in the lower sanctuary, he did speak
But the greetings were meek and weak, or not at all
I just sat there wondering why I'd come at all
Fear of what FATHER to me would say
Is what kept me from goin' Satan's way

In the upper sanctuary, the praise team did their thing
I sang along, clapping my hands and shifting my feet
Satan had no choice – he had to retreat!
The Spirit assured me I'm in a season
And have some, but not all GOD's reason.

He preached "The Perfect Storm" and I heard it many ways
But the Spirit in me, applied it this way…
'Holding on to your old ways gives Satan an area to play
You've been given a voice, along with a new one of GOD's choice
Best you take care, and lift up your voice
And bless others as I have blessed you
Or you'll continue to give the devil his due.'

How I Believe
May 12, 2007

'What is and is not a favorable outcome?'
'My salvation - Yes, but by whose means?'
'What have I done to try and maintain control?'
And 'How do I check what's at the root of my soul?'
The answer to these and many others,
Are based on just one more
And to answer it ALL THINGS must be explored
It's 'How on GOD do I believe?'

And as I've asked myself the rest
I remember this too –
There is no faith if and as, there is no testimony
Without first taking the tests
And as with Job, I believe
It's my countenance during those times
By which I'll be blessed

As I've answered, I considered
Exactly who HE is
And all for us HE does and did
I go even deeper, and consider still
How on HIM I believe and what it means
To and how I've witnessed HIS Spirit
And whether or not I can and do hear it
As well as how I'll answer on that day
For I believe those answers based only on what I believe
Without the whys I believe them
Will prove only how I did or didn't seek HIM
And in the end will determine if I'll see HIM
For I know without faith it's impossible to please HIM   Heb 11:6

How is it that I believe?
I believe as He has proven and proves to me
How in the world, I'm as HE desired me to be
Save my measured human imperfections
Stripped and naked before HIM
HE loves me nonetheless
For as HE is restoring my soul
I continue to relinquish my control
While in the world, it looks as if I've lost it
But knowing in GOD, I've actually found it
A peace which transcends even my own understanding
And a desire to continue still
Seeking HIM and for me, HIS will
Resting on HIS word, as HE spoke it – even unto me
And during those times, I couldn't and didn't see
It was always HIM who rescued me
Believing also that as HE makes me whole
HIS plans for me will unfold.

At Beautiful
May 12, 2007

Before the strike of the ninth hour
It's at Beautiful I was set
Brought there by the missionaries of GOD
And I'll never forget
Impeded by circumstances, almost since birth
It was HIS hidden Spirit that kept me on this earth

At the strike of the ninth hour
It was at Beautiful I set
There by GOD's mercy
And I'll never forget
Meekened, and humbled
Head bowed, and right hand extended
It was by the alms of HIS Spirit my stance corrected

Before the end of the ninth hour
It's through the gates of Beautiful I was moved
Embraced by GOD's Spirit, which brought me through

That Which I Seek
May 12, 2007

Through baptism, we are to become as Christ
As it is the cleansing of the soul
For me, it was the first day of my salvation
As in the world I'm now one without nation
Shedding those things not of GOD
Reliant upon HE and HIS grace
My new beginning has come to pass
However, it's not done
As I know now that which I seek
Salvation by HIS good and perfect grace
And at it's peak

For me, what's at the root of my soul
What keeps me from being out of control
Is the way, the truth, and the life
In this world I have nothing
Save my faith and obedience
Even as Christ – Not a place of my own
But I know now that which I seek
Is to be GOD's perfect peace
With Jesus keeping me sweet

My faith in GOD – HIS way, HIS truth
For me, it's HIS desired life
And I thank GOD for HIS will of days
My new beginning, though it is small
Is still larger than this worldly life
As I know now that which I seek
Is to be at GOD's throne
And at HIS right hand for me a seat.

I Am Her!
May 13, 2007

As it is - it is the field of faith that I do glean
Collecting the remnants of what is GOD's seed

Who am I, that I may stand before you
And tell you what I believe is true
I am her!
Her who halteth
And her who was driven out
Even her who hath been afflicted by HIM
Tested and pre-tested to measure the countenance within.

I who was given a name before my birth
Formed in and of the earth
And was driven out before I could realize my worth
Now halted as HE has called me by my given name
Causing me to remember from whence I came

Standing before you, the remnant of my former self
Strong in my faith, in which I have no shame
For I dwell in HIS heavenly place
Embraced by, and covered in the blood
Of HIS good, and perfect Grace. . .

YOUR Messengers?
May 28, 2007
Micah 4:1-8

Are YOUR messengers here GOD?
For I have no reason to fear,
The glimpses in my peripheral view,
I take comfort, because I only see them
When I'm communing with YOU.

Are YOUR messengers here GOD?
They seem quite busy,
What would YOU have them do?
Will they speak, or even touch,
Or are they preparing the next blessing
Because I trust YOU that much?
And have taken more steps
Out on faith's thin limbs
Believing YOUR strength is within them.

Are YOUR messengers here GOD?
They seem quite busy,
What would YOU have them do?
Are they here to prepare me for my next test,
Or are they just to remind me it's always been YOU?
I remember now only in hindsight,
And praise YOU, for YOU saw my plights.

Are YOUR messengers here GOD?
I have no fear
For even if not them
I know YOU're near

June 23, 2007

To my GOD in heaven,
What I've learned from YOU these last days
Is I want not, and cannot continue my old ways
To a world which had not, and still has none
And to those who had not enough of their own
I, who was of YOUR inspiration, before my birth
Formed in and of the earth,
Gave away my own self worth
And that which I stated I desired in the past
YOU've proven even my days it can't and won't out last
As YOUR wisdom in me, is coming into it's own
I can now wait for YOU to call me home.

Some my question how I've come to my conclusions
And may conclude my faith an illusion
But YOUR Spirit in me, has revealed my own truths
I forgave them, but not…
I trusted no one, not even…
At the end of both put 'myself'
And the list goes on, and some clichés
But I know this one is true, Satan has nothing on me,
For I have been my own worst enemy
I wasn't hiding from the world, as completely as from myself
Have mercy and forgive me FATHER
As now, I'm in the measure and the treasure
Of the Spirit YOU've dealt – once again in bloom
Relating, relating my current and former life
Peace and grace to those who came early
Along with visions to the blind
On all who seek HIM, GOD is equally kind.

By and for YOUR church
In and for the fellowship of YOUR Son
Not YOUR reason, but the means
To educate those who on YOU truly believe
In and on the fruits of the Spirit,
And the realization of dreams
Lessons learned and worldly things tossed aside,
From YOUR will for me, I can no longer hide
I can be of YOU and be as I dare to dream,
For simplistically speaking, what's not of YOU
Falls apart at the seams

For what the Spirit has, and keeps proving me
How in YOU and me I see
YOUR transcendental light –
Which purges the soul of world controls,
And also a passion ignites
To put up first YOURS
And then my own good fight.

The Reason For The Season
2007 Advent Devotional for Concord Baptist Church, Milton
July 7, 2007

Christ the perpetual reason for the yuletide season
Easily lost because we measure the costs of those things we bought
One day or season in and of the year
Christ-mas – A festival of Christ
Lost is the meaning of worship GOD
All the days of our life

From small beginnings, by GOD's will BE
The son of GOD and HIS true purpose for you and me
His Son given, not first nor last, but always
Because we don't escape our inherited ways

And for all this HIS anger is not turned away
But HIS hand is out stretched still
Welcoming all who seek HIM and HIS will.

PACTS With GOD
July 15, 2007

When I **P**raise GOD, it's from my soul and with my heart
And it's because HE's given me, each day a new start
In HIS will in and of me
As it pertains to HIS desire to see
All those HE's created in eternity

When I **A**sk GOD for anything, it's from my heart
And it's because I embrace saving faith with each new start
As pertains to Our vision of eternity
And those there We both hope to see

When I **C**onfess to GOD
I confess Christ and the cross
Claiming, naming, and repenting sin one and / and for all
As I see what is the excellence of Christ
And the will of GOD

When I **T**hank GOD
It's from my soul and with my heart
And it's because I continually receive a new part
In my faith in GOD, and in me too
As it pertains to the role HE has for me
In HIS vision of and plan for eternity

When I **S**erve GOD and mankind
It's from my heart and with my soul
For I have embraced the contract Spirit of the Sovereign GOD
Who's always been in control

Jesus Said – (Complacency Part II)
July 31, 2007

Jesus said, "…this is that bread that came down from heaven…
    he that eateth of this bread shall live for ever."
John 6:58

And I believe this to be true
Even as I'm stepping out of and back in too
'I'll do me, you do you'

Jesus said, "Labour…but for that meat which endureth unto
    everlasting life"
John 6:27

Meaning search the word and it's words
And HE by you shall be heard
And I know this to be true
Because I can share this with you

Jesus said, "Man shall not live by bread alone, but by every word
    which proceedeth out of the mouth of God"
Matthew 4:4

And I believe this to be true too
This is Complacency Part II
As even at that time I did see it,
But lacked the word on how He'd mean it
Man shall not live by bread alone
Can you see all that it means?
It's the difference between live for ever and everlasting life
As by me, it may be seen

The problem with for ever is that it does come
For it is the end of the chronicles of man
And everlasting life is where heaven actually began.

UNLAWFUL - ?
August 15, 2007

"All things are lawful for me, but all things are not expedient: all things are lawful for me, but edify not. Let no man seek his own, but every man another's wealth."
I Corinthians 10:23, 24

All things lawful, but not all expedient
Means the wrong path chosen,
GOD's blessings not immediate
All things lawful, but edify not
Means your path and mine are all we've got

I judge not another's path, as I know my rite it's not
I cast lots only to ensure it's HIS Spirit I've got
I'd much rather we discuss all the promises GOD's made to us
And why we believe as we do
For I know if we do that
GOD won't bless just one, but two

It's not your Spirit, nor is it mine
The fact that we have it makes us two of a kind
And the discussion ensures us we're not Spiritually blind

Some may say it's enough just to believe
And to that I say, heaven is a place of degrees
And our inheritance there is based on the individual GOD sees.

IT Too
August 18, 2007

IT's in our faces, more specifically our eyes
IT's in our hearts, more specifically our sighs
IT's not a tangible, something we may touch
But IT's our dignity being drained from us.

Where is the compassion for our fellow man?
Asked while I'm embraced by GOD's unfailing hand
While I give HIM all praise and thanks for who I am
Though not receiving, but keeping my own respects
As I'm homeless and treated like a suspect
I call on Jesus early in the day, that I may find peace
And even He sometimes finds it hard to keep me sweet

I can't find the words to express how I really feel
As I thank the Lord for keeping me near
And tell Him I can't wait to get out of here
Lost in the world, but not in HIS word
It is Christ Jesus that I heard, telling me to hold on
For in my weakness, He is strong

I pray also if this be my testimony
O' Lord, may I please past this test
For that which emphasizes it's difficulty
Is most around me aren't spiritually blessed

As I see IT, a part of what HE desires of me
Is not to let the world take, or I give away
All that HE has promised me.

Untitled 8
September 9, 2007

I sometimes feel, but worry not
That it is HIM who may have me forgot
I lean on HIS word, which gives me nerve
To seek not what I want, but only deserve

In a world which covets it's own
I long to see that which is truly home
But I continue, yet and still
To drink of HIS water to swallow this pill

The pain of life, all but gone
As broken bones do mend
It's the state of and for my heart and mind
When I say "Amen, Amen, and Amen"

Giving HIM thanks for bringing me out from where I'd been
And the freedom given me in my pen
Taking me down to see and regain,
That which I, for so long did and have missed
All the while remembering my soul, has of heaven kissed
When Jesus lifted me up from this abyss
And blessed me with the fruits of the Spirit
I praise GOD – For HE my soul, still hears it.

Useful Idiots
October 3, 2007

Useful once upon a time - filled with Spirit
Influenced by the world
And now they barely hear it
It's a feeding frenzy in minds and the medias
As battle lines are drawn, and the wars waged
Then theorized in immature minds where Satan still plays

Useful idiots trained to be this way
Thought of by themselves to be okay
Non-heros cause stampedes to and for fame
Twisting the knowledge of a true hero's previous claim
And alienating the people and land from which they came
Further removed from that which was given before they saw a day
Useful idiots trained to think the wrong way
Not realizing it's guilt that causes them to stray
And not redeeming the time as evil is the day

Useful idiots believing they know all
Sometimes cause others to excuse GOD's call
Captivating young minds with what is the world's truth
Not realizing it's also GOD's Truth
'Nation against nation, brother against brother
Mothers and daughters pitted against one another

Useful idiots mis-behaving having not learned
It's the truth of the Sovereign GOD
And HIS will in which they should be concerned

Useful idiots could be me, could be you
It's all in the division we do

Our Shoes
October 9, 2007

I've considered the similarities
Between them and us
I've compared the personalities and such
I have even ear hustled a time or two
Trying to understand the complexities of me and you
Connected by a lifetime experience
But ever changed is a conscious choice

When you look at me, what do you see?
And how is it you perceive me to be?
A victim of circumstance,
Or the circumstance of a victim?
Either way I still need HIM
So when I look at you, I try to see HIM
As I search to find some kind or reason
To perceive in you of HIM I seek
Limited by my general knowledge in and of you
I tell myself, 'I can't do a mile in your shoes'
Losing what I may have gained,
When I took upon me the Son of man's name

It's with His thoughts I close my eyes at night
And say my ACTS
Knowing that I am just like you
And have already many miles in your shoes
For an addiction of any kind is still the same
And as victory is it's own reward
Life on earth a double edged sword
But as I ask HE restores my soul
As I try to lose and maintain all control.

Jesus Had To Pray
February 26, 2008

After the breaking of bread
And the cup passed around
After the hymn sung
They all moved to higher ground

It was there at Gethsemane
Jesus had to pray for you and me
Jesus, Peter, John and James on the mount
If you should die, then I should too   Matt 26:35
We'll drink of the cup God would have you   Matt 20:21, 22
Earlier oaths of them that slept seemingly slip away
Nevertheless, "not as I will, but as thou wilt"
Jesus on the Mount of Olives had to pray

The spirit indeed willing, but the flesh is weak
The acceptance of us is what He speaks
His soul sorrowful even unto death
He knew before He prayed what is our best
"If this cup may not pass, except I drink it"
Jesus on the Mount of Olives had to pray
Lest all hope be lost even unto this day

All the while His soul weeped
Peter, John and James remained asleep
"If this cup may not pass, except I drink it "
On the mount at Gethsemene
Jesus had to pray for you and me
As the cup now passed, to each man not his own
And GOD has long ago called HIS Son to HIS throne
If Jesus had to pray for us at Gethsemane
Why shouldn't we be on bended knees
Praying for those after, and forgiving them before we?

From Faith to Faith
March 2008

One GOD, one faith, one Spirit
That is how I believe
And all are descendants of Abraham's seed
As it is man who does measure
It is man who diminishes his own spiritual treasure
For GOD's will for the whole human race
Is salvation, ultimately by HIS good and perfect Grace
Knowing these things makes me ponder HIS day
When we will atone for all our ways

From faith to faith, what I think that means
It doesn't matter to GOD how on HIM you believe
For all faiths are on the same mission
It is man that continually fails at GOD's commission
To spread HIS truth and HIS wealth
And to make whole the human heart
Which is of dust or clay
It depends only on the version of HIS word you're reading today

Often ignored, unnoticed or even destroyed
GOD's true gifts to and of mankind
Because it is man that is still spiritually blind
For the truth of my GOD
And not only I may see
HE chose the world, as HE intended it to be
And used a nation as a demonstration of the power HE holds
Our misunderstanding brought about the misconceptions
Now spiraling out of control

Why is it that when some look not like me
It's only that they see
Rather than the uniqueness bestowed by HIM upon me?

Why is it, that when some do look like me
Without knowledge of
Others attempt to classify us
I am not this if I am of that
I am not that if I am of this
I say a crucial lesson has been missed
For my GOD created man
In the image and likeness of HIM
Male and female created HE them
Man termed himself 'hu'man
Which, alienated the origin of his birth
And humans spread inhumanity across the earth

Believing we first, and or better than another
When it matters not to GOD your denomination or skin color
As GOD is omnipotent, and omnipresent
Thus amongst every nation
So it doesn't even matter to GOD your location

The 'hu' in man that I do see
Are the impure colors of the souls of men,
Who think they're HE
As the lesson ignored, unnoticed or not taught at all
Don't forget, but forgive
And continue HIS fight that we may live.

The Battlefield
April 28, 2008

On the battlefield adorned in the armor of GOD
And humbled by the presence of HIM
I know it's not by might, nor by power,
  but by HIS Spirit I'll win   Zech 4:6
I have to listen closely, that I may hear it
As the belt of truth brings my inward stripes
It's the heart against the mind that fights
For my heart is where my GOD does rest
Protected by the breastplate of HIS righteousness
As it is HE and HIS wisdom that I do seek
Yet sometimes my countenance grows weak
But I'm protected by the helmet of salvation
So even if my boots get muddied
And HIS peace seems not to be found,
My shield of faith and the sword of HIS word
Are enough to bring strongholds down.
And as they crumble, I'm even more humbled
By the new horizon I peep
As it's me in HIM and HIM in me
HE assures me I see.

Under The Lily Whites
May 15, 2008

Under the lily whites where only GOD and I know
How white really my raiment glows
Standing in judgment of all I see
I realize I stand really in judgment of me

Am I who HE intended me to be?
Have I embraced all that I can be?

Under the lily whites where the spirit abodes
The winds of change blow hot and cold
Fleeing thoughts – No heed to convictions
Success sometimes for Satan's mission

Have I made a right choice?
Did I consult my CREATOR?..
Time will tell others, sooner or later

Under the lily whites where only GOD knows
What seeds are planted, and how they will grow

Anyoneofus – Prodigal Children
July 12, 2008

Anyoneofus children, those without face
Distrusted by man and the human race
Not seen daily, for we cross the street
Or shift our eyes, dare we meet or even greet
Having forgotten that we have no fear
And it's the love of GOD we are to share
It's even our own cries for help we don't hear
Moving to the beat of our own drum
Our compassion poor-s out only as we lose one

Anyoneofus children, those without faith
Dedicated to a life predicated on waste
Products of the 'hu in man' race
None should wonder how or why they are lost
For those who have come unto GOD's Light
Should know it's for the prodigal children we fight
For the Son came not just for you and me
As all sin was nailed to that tree
Christ in us, we are Him
Called to bring the light of GOD unto them

The prodigal children of GOD are we all
But we'll only be humbled and changed
When we heed HIS call.

In Beginnings
October, 2008

In the beginning, there was GOD
The heaven and all the earth
HIS word and Spirit performed
HIS table prepared before I was born
In the beginning, there was GOD
But I knew HIM not.

In my beginning, there was in me a bright light
But I was unaware it's not mine own
At a time when discontents and malcontents freely roamed
Well lit places became darkened public alleys and combat zones

Equal rights, segregation, and what about Indians on reservations
Too many wars in and of just one nation
"Make Love Not War" and "God Is Love"
Slogans thought to be from above
Clung to mostly by the carnal on drugs
Parochial schools and religion classes
Taught by some in need of teaching
While others forgot on Sunday's they are preaching

World problems weighed heavy on my mind
I had wonders but no signs
There's no sound doctrine, just the blind
Which in turn were leading me to be blind

Oblique and sly, snide remarks
Jaded secrets and unwanted touch
Nocturnal dreams ended by a mother's screamed pleas
This nightmare was my reality
On the morrow blackened and bloodshot eyes are all I'd see

In the beginning, there was GOD
But before I learned my light was of HIM
The light itself in me went dim
For what is a nation or even a family
When and if there's no unity
And what's in a name depends on how and by whom you've been called it
My name is, therefore I am
And not one of you has to like it!
As an owner of a tortured soul and battered spirit
The light called to me, but I pretended not to hear it

A wallflower even in my own mind
As I daydreamed and left myself and the world behind
And often under the twists of trees
I searched the world and myself
To find some rhyme or reason for undue seasons
And to perceive what is my truth
Wasted days are the culmination of my youth.

Partiality, partial and whole truths
Kept me from taking up my own roots
Much older now, and indifferent
As the world cannot define me
For it holds not what I seek
As I partook of all dominions and principalities
And resisted those authorities
I came to this realization…
In that world there was just me
For none that I know lived it as me

Blown with the wind, while swimming against the waves
Despair continued to fill my days
Having tried everything else,
'I know I need GOD'
So I humble myself, and go to HIM meek
And before HIM, I slaughter the beast
Then my confession I begin to speak
And tell HIM it's heaven on earth that I seek

In the beginning, there was GOD
Just as HE's always been
With outstretched hands,
Waiting for me to turn and honor HIM

In my beginning, there was GOD
A bright light in what seemed to be a non-existent place
The FATHER removing the remnants of mud from HIS child's face.

And I Know, I Know
May 22, 2009

Well rested, as I did sleep
In my actions, my body did find peace
I know I seek these two -
Heaven on earth, and to fully realize my worth
And I know, I have other desires...

I know GOD only, can and will measure
HIS truth in and of my heart
So evermore careful am I, in the things that I start
I consider everything, and try not to worry for any
For I know GOD does take care of HIS own
Yet sometimes I wonder
If I'm reaping what I've elsewhere sown
And I know I've changed some attitudes
Thereby altering all perceptions
And I know too, that all shall see
What is and isn't of GOD in me

I know I believe that in my faith I am not alone
And I know it's a delicate, soul searching matter
But if I am alone, this too I must see
I can't help being the spirited social misfit
GOD created me to be.

This supposes that I fear the judgment of others
But I know I fear GOD's judgment of them
And I know, what I do in their sight
Even if from my heart
Is how GOD's judgment of me will be brought
For I know, if one stands in judgment of another
What they do, think, say,
Have done and will do
I know it will condemn that one too.

I know I trust GOD first
To my heart HE does speak
So if my heart replies, are my words lies?
As they model my desires
I know GOD's laws
And I know it's HIS inspiration I see in me
Which simply stated is to BE!
Devoted to HIM and on top in my world
Or do I really want it all re-versed
And really desire to put myself first?

Nay! - I desire first to give myself to GOD
But and still to one of the earth
I know they cannot, nor will they ever be equal
Nor too are they the same
As I see one in the earth
But I know from whence he came
And I know he is a gift of GOD to me
Even before I learn his name
One with understanding of these things few
The fear and knowledge of GOD
As well as the differences in and of twos
And his own motives behind
All he did, does and will do
One man cut from my same cloth
A weaving of faith and flesh
As my desires are both selfless and of my flesh
One who in the likeness of GOD
Aspires himself and inspires me
To be all that GOD intended us to be

I know by GOD, all things have reasons
And I know to redeem the time, means to seize the seasons
For I know what's of GOD to me, will prove to last
And it will be even after my time has passed
But should I have hope only in then
And not move on earth for what I seek of heaven
And what's in heaven that I should seek

Mere words are not nigh to my conception
But I know to say this is a close exception
"All things back to GOD!
Or as HE wills it, a re-collection of HIM
And in the fires of hell are only our sins"

I know I cannot actually or accurately measure
In another, GOD's spiritual treasures
So I go only by what GOD does prove to me
It's how I know, HE loves and watches over me
And I know it is GOD that truly inspires
My not so natural desire
To demonstrate HIS love in and of me
And to share with all, and one - HIS bounty
So if I give to one, and only him
What's of no use to GOD in heaven
Is it still a sin against GOD?
Even if that one is and does feel the same
And in this neither has any shame?

I know the one I desire, the one of the same cloth
Is the one in which I won't be lost
And I know if I take that which I know is GOD given
None on earth may judge
For I know I took it in, by and for the reason of GOD's love

If by reading you don't know what this is
I will tell you what it be
It's the introverted, retrospective view
Of what I desire in, for, and from you.

An Agape Type Thing
July 2009

To the fruit of the womb
All I can say is I did and do my best
In giving you what I have that you may need less

I trust you completely - That's from the start
And give you the world, as it is mine to give
That your needs not surpass how you live
Nothing you have done or will do
Could ever make me stop loving you
For everything you think you guilty of - I am too!
Therein is the reason I still believe in you.

To know yourself and your needs
Is to know that in my world you can be pleased
As what I offer you is a lifetime of love
The question is 'Is will you take it
And be ever careful not to break it?'
Knowing to whom much is given
From them the more it is expected
As the gift of love should not be neglected.

Yet all are different, but and still the same
So as I give you the best of what's in and of me first
It is you who determines if it's of worth
The value of which is established in your own hearts and eyes
So when and while you are thinking of yourself
I hope you remember me too
And know I never lied to you
For I can only do and be in your world
Only as you ask me to.

Duality - More Than ONE - Equal to Two
July 2009

I don't really want to die here on earth
So I have hope in the rapture
But I do long to see home
My beginning as GOD let's me see
Was truly in the heart of HE
My GOD is my inspiration, and my reason
I stand bare, and bear witness to my own duality
And as I write, I know I feel the quickening of me

I am of GOD!
None may deny, and that includes even I
For I was there almost from the beginning
I am the son of the sixth day
The first of my own kind
I am GOD's Son of man
Perfect in my generation
As I am still in HIM
For I was molded in HIS thoughts first
In the image and likeness of Them
I am the truth of GOD, by the definition of HIS word
And I know HIS Spirit resides in me
For it was the Spirit that did breathe life into me.

I am of the world
As it is where GOD created all I see and may see
And put in the care of me
At the root of my soul, I know that includes me
For I am the crown jewel of HIS creation
One GOD, plus One Spirit equals One Nation
But I lost HIS order and my place in my translation
I am the son of the morning I thought I could seize control
Of heaven here on earth
As I thought that as HE placed me here first

It should all revolve around me
This is the day I became my own worst enemy
And gave birth to inhumanity
As the views and hues of man emerged within me
My desires continued to divide, separate and conquer me.

Fast forward to a time there was just me
I know it was GOD who told me
"The world is mine!"
This was the day HE named me 'Meek'
That until an appointed time I shall not speak
Then of the bread of adversity and water of affliction
I too must eat
So that I may recognize my true TEACHER
And see HIS truth in me.

Hope Laid Up
October 23, 2009

"For the hope which is laid up for you in heaven, whereof ye heard before in the word of the truth of the gospel;"
Colossians 1:5

I wished it weren't so, and I hoped I wouldn't be
What others thought of, or thought they perceived in me
Then the traditions had not yet taken hold
As I battled outside forces, my enemy plotted courses
My hope then, was just to get through
As I couldn't see beyond early circumstances, I just knew
"I don't want to be like any of you!"
Defiance taught by and in the ways of man
The truth is! Even if it's in deceit
It's the inherent knowledge
That makes the liars out to be of man
Transient peace found in solitude
But only when not thinking of self as non-existent
For in that place there's only echoed silence
Witnessed is the dead amongst the living
My hope then, that there would be more to life
Than that which I may do or see
As I can't find my passion, yet it yearns to be free
Taught that GOD sees all, I still have hope HE sees me

The dawning of my faith is in the fear
That HE would be just like you, and overlook me too
Hope exercised my patience, as I learned HIS truth
And ALL THINGS are in the reflection
The truth is because I seek it
And nothing touched by man remains unchanged
Inclusive of GOD and me
My hope then, GOD is _____
And on my own will I fill in the blank

For my own traditions are firmly in place
And I don't trust or believe in any race
Either of man, or even faith
As I know GOD is not religion!
My survival is GOD's intercessions
Yea, even HIS mercy
For faith cometh by the hearing of the Word
And how I hear it is in me, as I battle with my enemy
Revealing the renting of my heart and soul
HE who has ears heard, and HIS eyes did see
As things in the world came and went easily
Unmoved in my stance and in discourse, was me
My hope then, was still that GOD will see
What really is in and at the heart of me

The coming of Christ was on this wise
A defining moment
The truth of HIS word as I can and do see
It's the resurrection of the Son of man in me
For GOD's word does not return to HIM void
My hope laid up in heaven , will always be
GOD's re-collection of me to HE.

Now
November 7, 2009

Only in faith can all truth be revealed
Thus in GOD all life makes sense
For it is the legacy of HIM
Initially taught by the understanding of men
The truth of HIS word is what I seek
Both in how it was written
And how HE now speaks it to me
Hide me Jesus in these truths
"He who would save his life shall lose it"
And in my weakness are you strong
For in this battle I'll not survive on my own.

Having claimed my own duality
In a darkened room I now ponder my faith
Questioning if I am even worthy of HIS love
As I consider previous choices
I can of the past, hear all voices
It comes again early - mid summer
My harvest season
And I shall reap all that I've sown
Yet now the field of faith becomes the battle
As it is my comfort zone
The borders of which by GOD are expanded

Now, as and in alway
These things doth my GOD hate
A proud look, a lying tongue
And hands that shed innocent blood
A heart of wicked imaginations
Feet swift into mischief
And a false witness
And even he that sows discord
Some if not all are to me known
The beginnings of my own reasoning in and of life
Prepare now to battle for control.

Now beyond my harvest
In what is the same darkened space
Strong men lay in wait
That they may slay me
Before I can take possession of the promised lands of HE
Men of valor, both young and of old
And who have tasted previously of the spoils of war

Now as I approach, embracing my faith
I know by GOD I am approved
For it is the light of HIS countenance
That comes shining through
Laying waste to the darkness of fear and doubt
It is for HIS victory I give praise and shout
For it is the pride of those men that caused their fall
As GOD's truth sets the oppressed and all others free
To testify to the faithfulness, longsuffering, and forgiveness of HE

Now even greater is HE that is within me
As my heart reflects of HIM all that I have received
This 'Now' as in all HIS works
Is my submission and remembrance to HE
For by GOD's grace, and other's faith
The King of kings saved me

Now commissioned and committed to Christ's cause
The direct line to ALL TRUTH
I write 'Now' not for the saving of myself
But that through my faith now
HE may save others before and after me too.

Measured Distance
March 6, 2010

Measured is the distance between us
And the distance is in the times
Of which no man is in control
In 'ours is not to reason why'
Is the courage and strength it takes to stand alone
While patience has her perfect work.

Measured is the distance between us
And the distance is in the times
So if I said nothing then
It's because I had nothing to say to you
Words on deaf ears are wasted
So why waste both our times?

In the measured distance are our reasons
For the things we say and do
As was and is my desire to reach out and try to know you
For back in the day, I was never moved
Because from you I had no need
Please correct me if I'm wrong,
But you felt and feel the same way too
Because I can't recall, and neither will you
When you first extended your hand in fellowship to me.

In the measured distance are our perceptions of self and others
Where one can conceive and believe they can see something in another
But cannot see it in themselves
The evidence is in the words we do and don't use
And the manner in which they are delivered
Out and even in their context, the views are skewed
So neither of us may ever know all truth.

In the measured distance are our beliefs
GOD's word heard and preached
The foolishness of which I can and do understand
Is that any need to be preached to at all
As knowledge of GOD is inherent,
For to say GOD is anything, is to know that HE is
But it's HIS wisdom that reveals all distances are HIS

Immeasurable are the distances in and of all GOD's firsts
Inclusive of what and when HE first spoke to me
The evidence of my measure is in "with WHO's eyes
Have I seen and do see all things?"
As well as, with who's authority I speak when I tell you
"If you have come to lie in HIS green pastures,
Then know you've been lead to come along side me.
As I am the voice of the stilled water, GOD created to run deep
And my soul's purpose is to help you keep HIS pastures green."

November 17, 2010

Righteous judgment is absent of self
But not at its own expense
Our hopes in the world are based on
The inspirations and aspirations
To be and have all things
GOD's FAITH is the POWER needed to BE ALL THINGS

The Child Doesn't Speak

Who would tell of the truth in a child's HOPE
If the child does not speak
And what should it matter to her the cause
In the eyes of any - Save GOD's
The burdens of youth are heavy!

Referenced are the descriptive details
In which life in the world reveals itself
Recognized are they as unseen from the beginning
Rebellion - I will not think, believe, or always do as
Any would have, ask, or even expect me to!
Defiance - I will not think or believe I am as, or even different from Any Other.

The generation of faith is the Spiritual Order of course
And in this child's view, and not of course
The first hope is to be as Enoch!
Who walked with GOD, and then he was not!
For GOD took him!

And with respect given to ALL referenced TIMES
The concept, not the reason is what is so pleasing
But as a point of reference all before him, most after him,
And frankly even Jesus Christ died!

The scriptures though inspired by GOD
Are nonetheless steeped in the traditions of men
Thus the generation of faith is often stilled
In the perceptions of, and by those seen before
Nonetheless, in GOD wills and does HIS child seek
The faith in and of her first HOPE

Complete Faith
January 22, 2011

If I were to tell you of a different perspective, even understanding
Regarding faith and what all may believe
Referencing a store bought book called the KJV
And words given by GOD's inspiration and aspiration
In and of me
Would you be shook, or would you see
The love of GOD towards you and me?

Reference Genesis 1:1
"In the beginning GOD - STOP!
Really, is there any need to say more
Except to say, I understand how we think
And know it's not the entire verse
As it continues to go on to say
Even before HE spoke a word
"...created the heaven and the earth"
Yes! This is about how HE's always revealed it to me
And "In the beginning GOD" now throughout
the entire store bought book is all I see
As with this statement is my testament of HIS SOVEREIGNTY
'If GOD never spoke a word, HE would GOD be,
And in HIM and still, would be ALL THINGS

Thus any understanding is of GOD
And the son of man HE generated first
Conceived in GOD's SPIRIT, by HIS Word
In the image and likeness of them
Eternal life and all truth were and still are of GOD's first fruits

Add them to the multi colored, jewel encrusted crown of
HIS creation
Spirit, Body and Soul
Created in ONE MIND and in ONE SPIRIT
By the will of GOD
But as the firsts of our kinds failed, so too do the rest
For even in our faith we walk stilled by our sight
As man continues to ignore his generations
Getting caught up or lost in his own translations
The repetition of them is a perpetual mindset
Of mind, body and soul
As we make ALL THINGS subject to our flesh
GOD will forever put HIS self destructive creation HUMANITY
To the test
For in "In the beginning GOD" this too I see
ALL THINGS means ABSOLUTELY EVERYTHING
Is still under HIS control

The revelation was this truth
There can be no hope in the end, if you don't know the beginning
And I have always found rest in GOD
So as I traced my origin and yes, even my earthly roots
I can see most, if not ALL TRUTH
And know all firsts belong to and are of GOD
And I am content with the wisdom that knowledge includes me
For in "In the beginning GOD" this too I see
I didn't choose GOD, but from the beginning HE chose me
Not as I am, but as HE created me to be.

Now before I take you to where I am going
I will show you where it began in accordance
to my confession of faith
And my relationship to ALL THINGS,
Reference

"And be not conformed to this world, but be ye transformed by the renewing of your mind, that ye may prove what is that good, and acceptable, and perfect will of GOD"
Romans 12:2 in the store bought book
I know for some, the relativity is a stretch
But when I consider ALL THINGS, I consider ABSOLUTELY EVERYTHING
I know of both GOD's SPIRIT and our flesh
And it may well be, I set my hope too high
Seemingly overshadowing my example in Jesus Christ the Son of man
Who in both the Word, and in The End
Has His own multiplicity
The understanding is in both
His entire ministry and the life He chose to lead

The Gospel of GOD's Truth
Jesus Christ, the Word of GOD manifested in the flesh
His way was GOD reliant as He always
acknowledged and represented by WHOM He was sent

His truth is we don't really prove GOD because HE proves HIMSELF
From ALL our BEGINNINGS and to ALL our ENDS
In accordance to our own faith

And Jesus' life was in obedient service and contentment
Because He knew His heavenly place.

Jesus, the Son of man was a man of GOD
Which in and by it's definition
"Is the man who judges ALL THINGS; yet he himself shall not be judged'
And He said,

"Think not that I am come to send peace on earth; I came not to send peace but a sword"
Reference Matthew 10:34
And later "I will draw all men unto me"
The operative word is 'unto' not 'into' is how I see
And that's really all the proof I need
To understand salvation is not His guarantee

For just as the Word of GOD was given flesh becoming the Son of man
He studied Himself perfecting ALL the generations of FAITH that were before Him
And because of it Jesus knew, as a man He had no heaven or hell to put any into
For He recognized Himself as not the AUTHOR, but hoped in GOD WHO did create
And GOD approved Him to be the 'cornerstone' and the epitome of what it is to have
COMPLETE FAITH

And as surely as I believe Jesus burden is our sin
I know this much is also true...

GOD's burden is still HIS Word
In and of both me and you.